WANT TO STEP UP YOUR PROSPERITY? YOU NEED TO COLOR THIS FIRST

ADULT COLORING BOOK

MY COLORING LAB

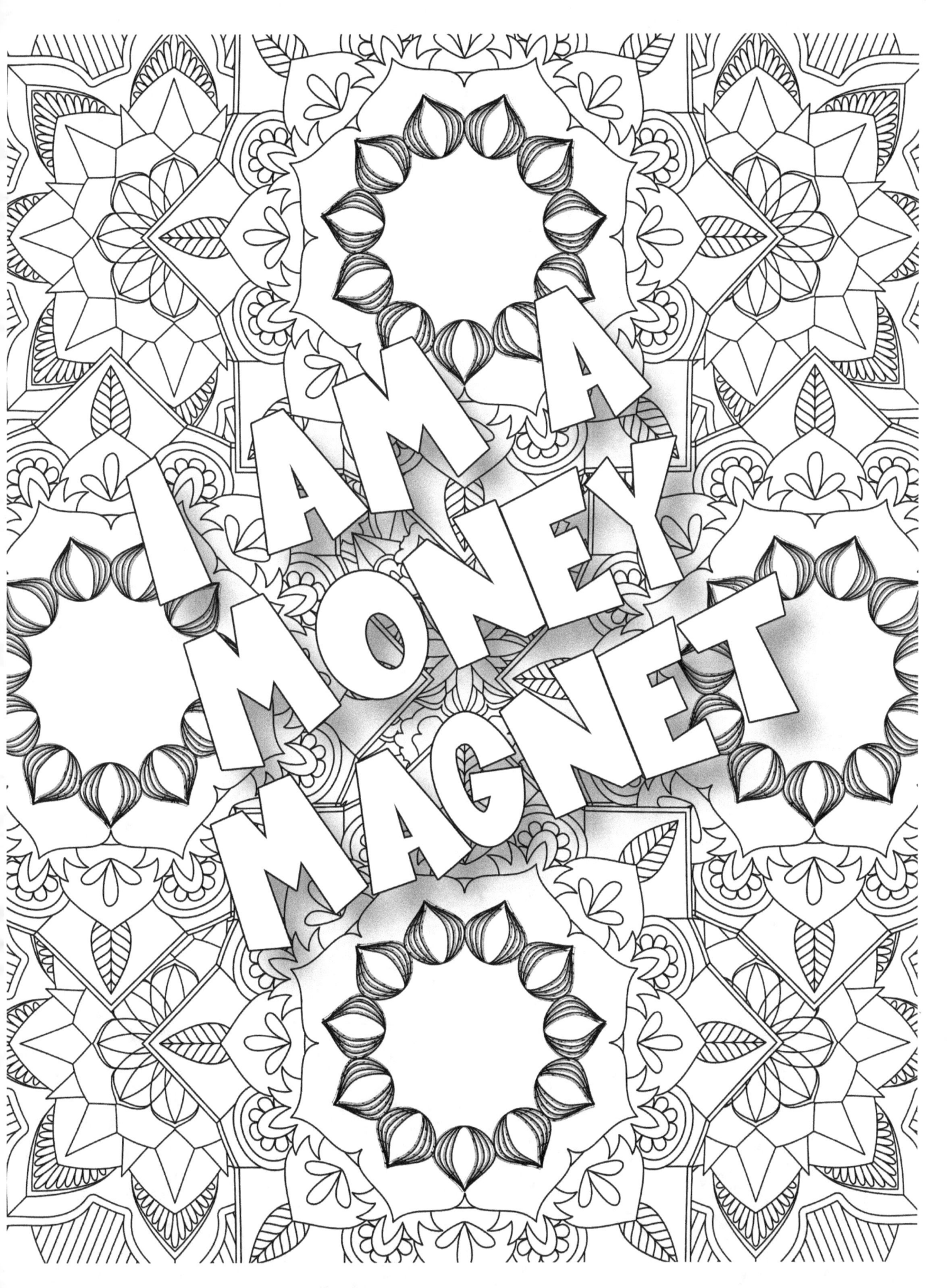

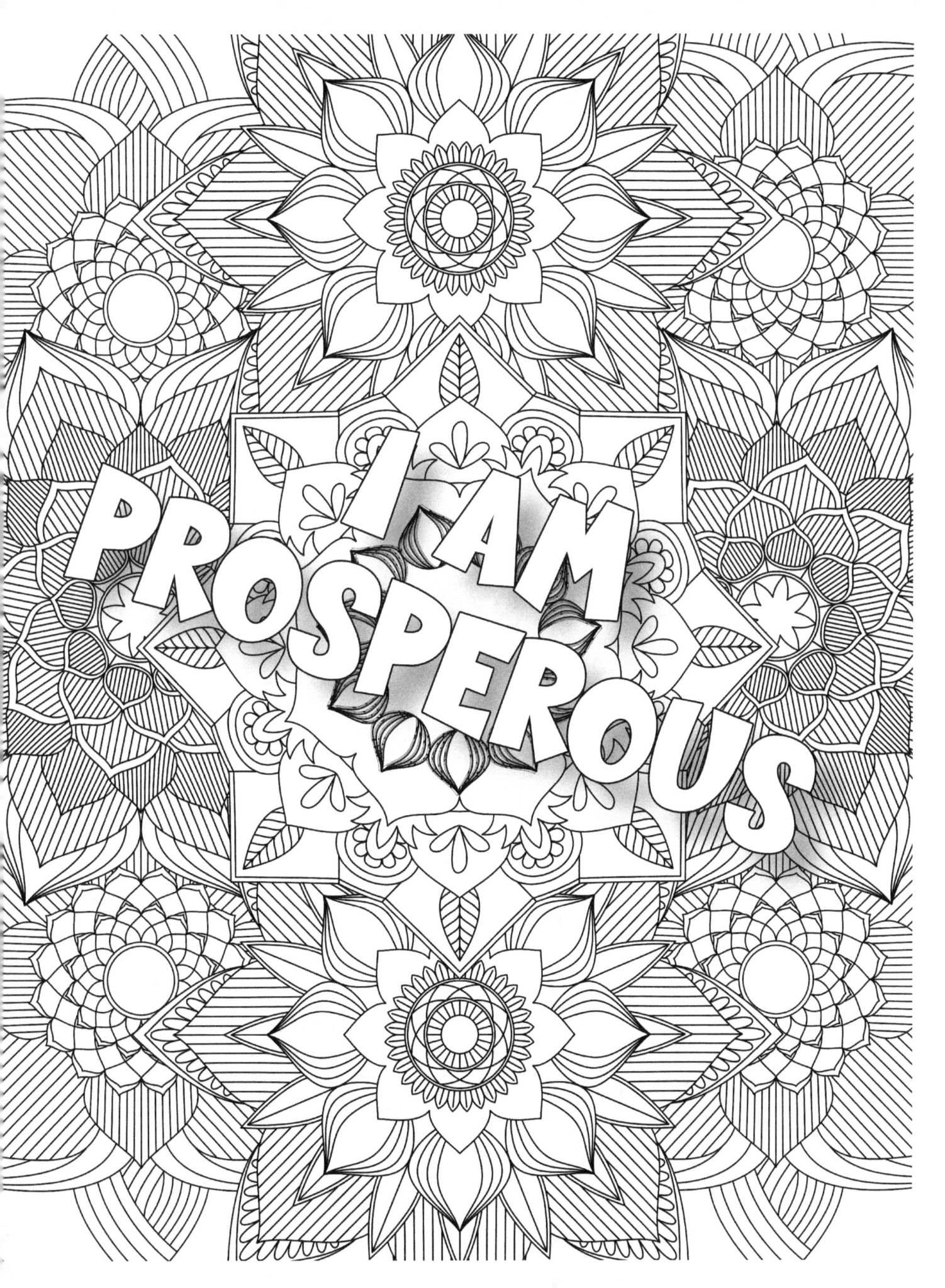

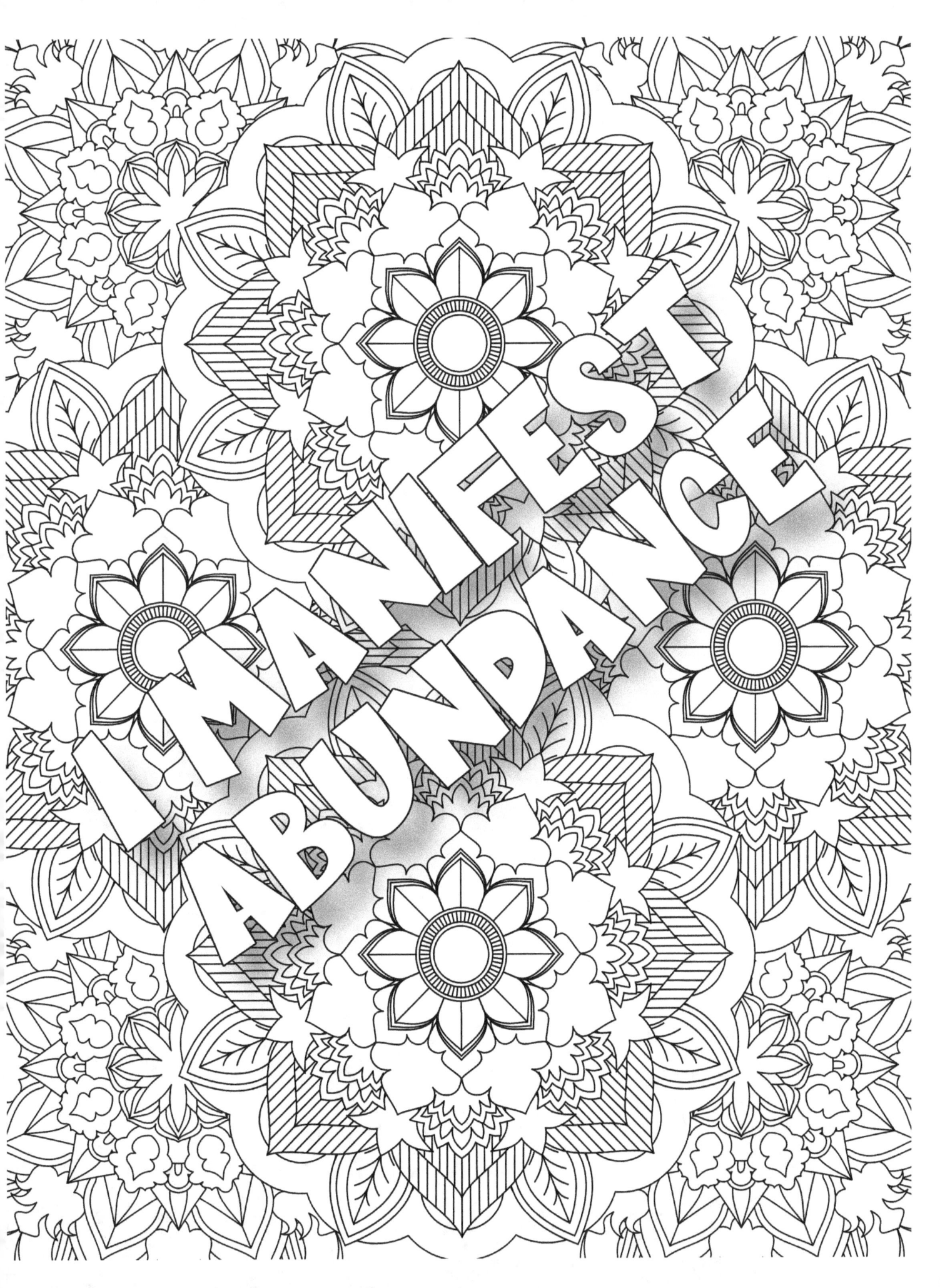

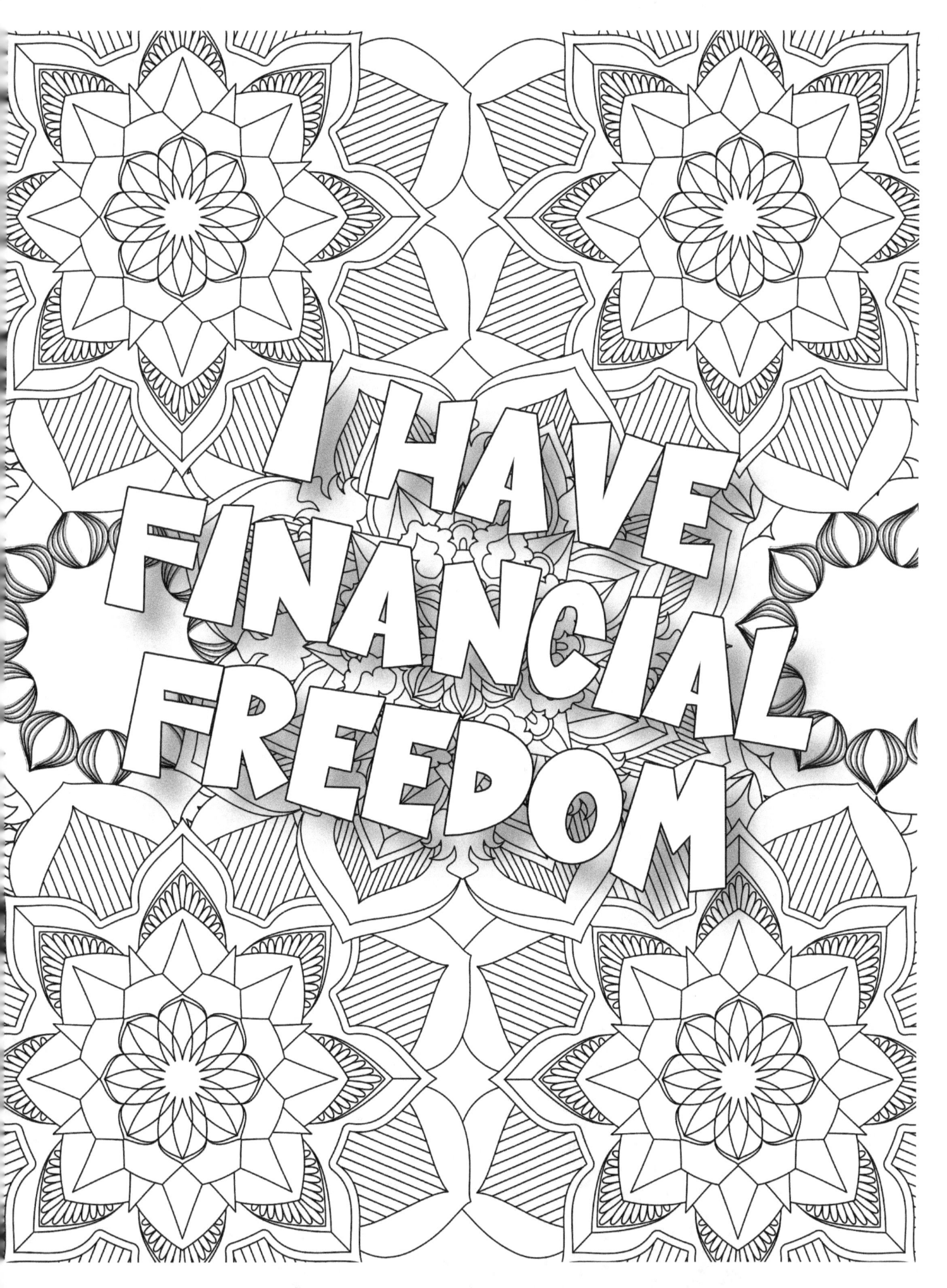

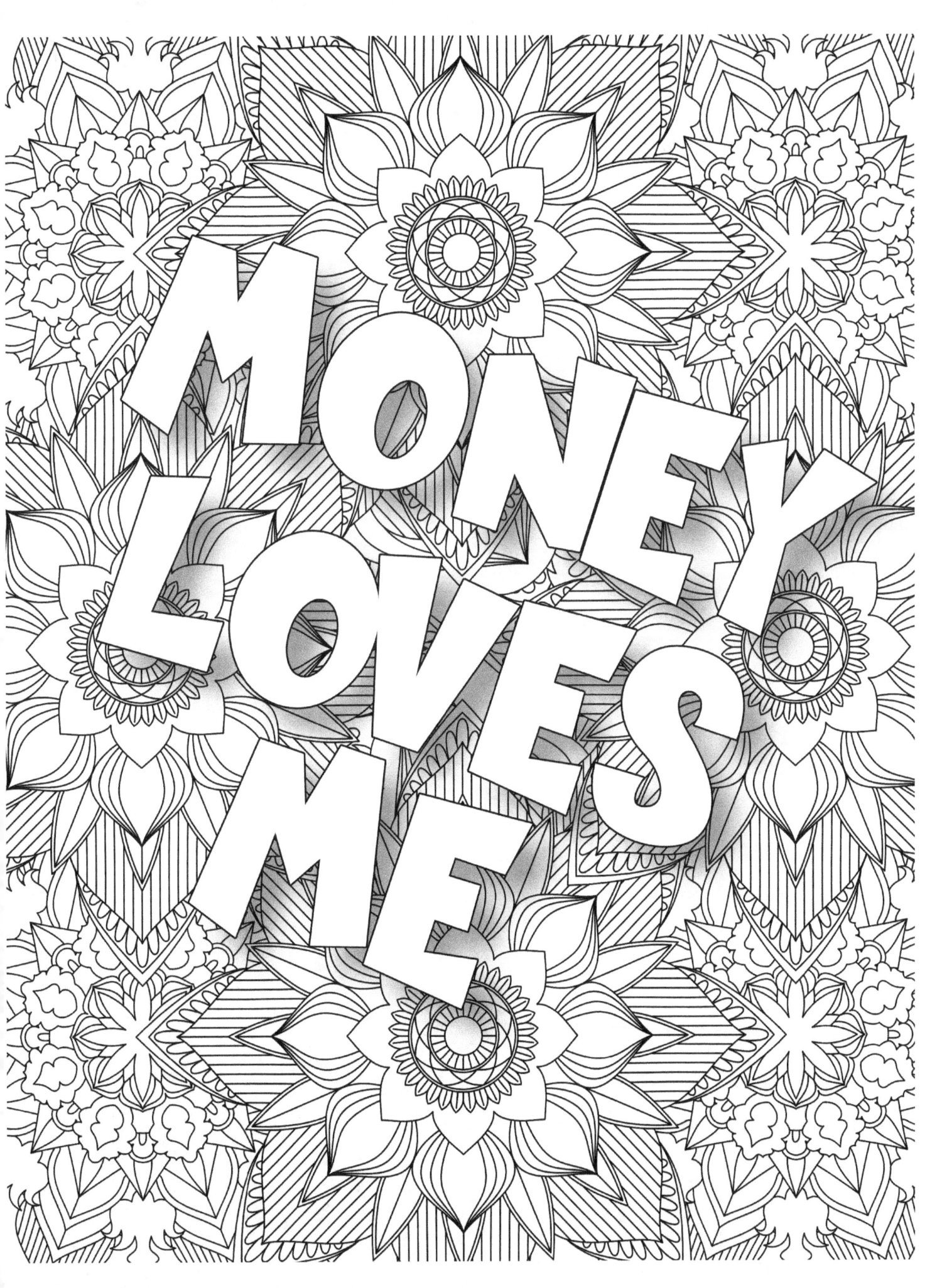

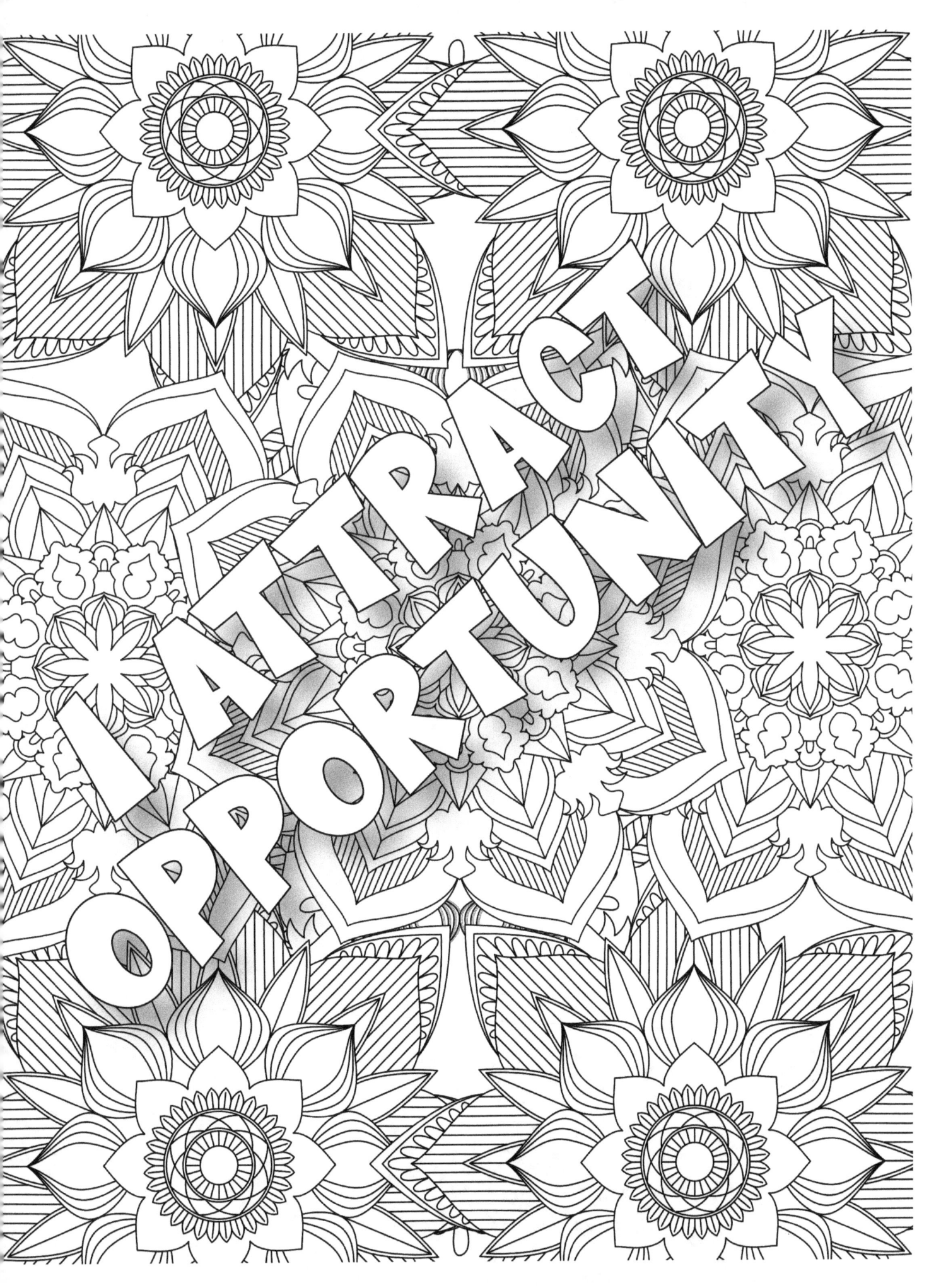

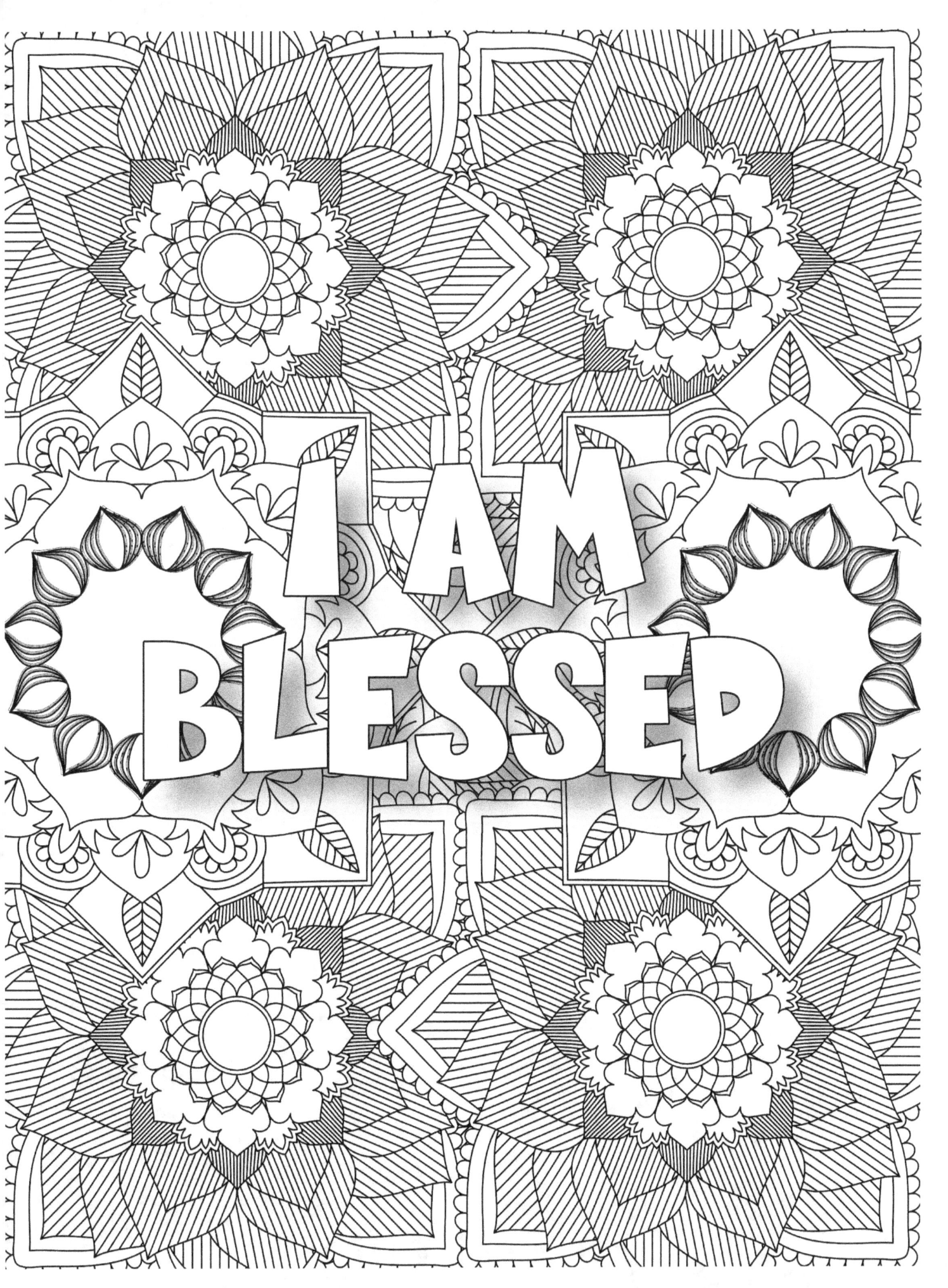

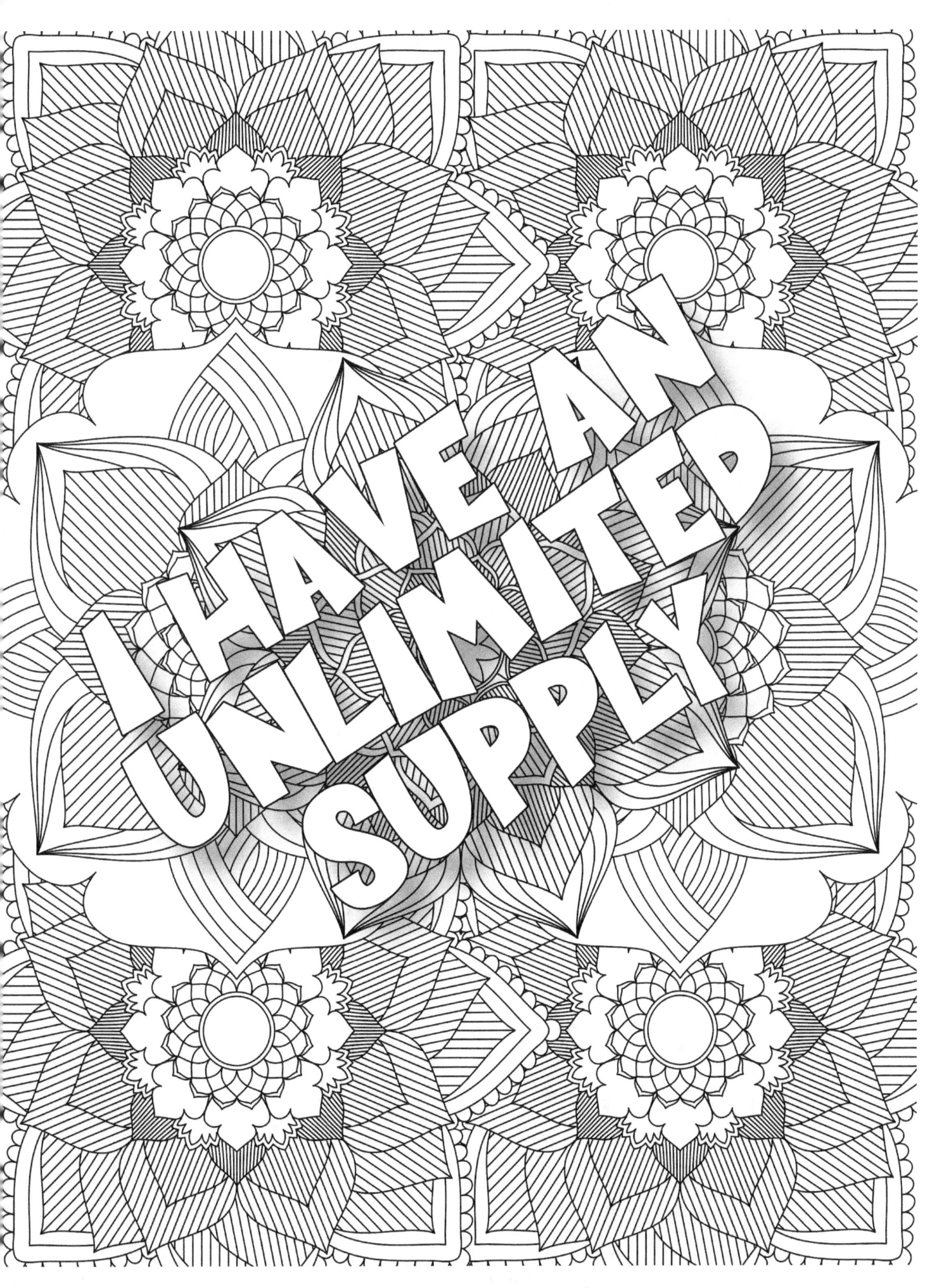

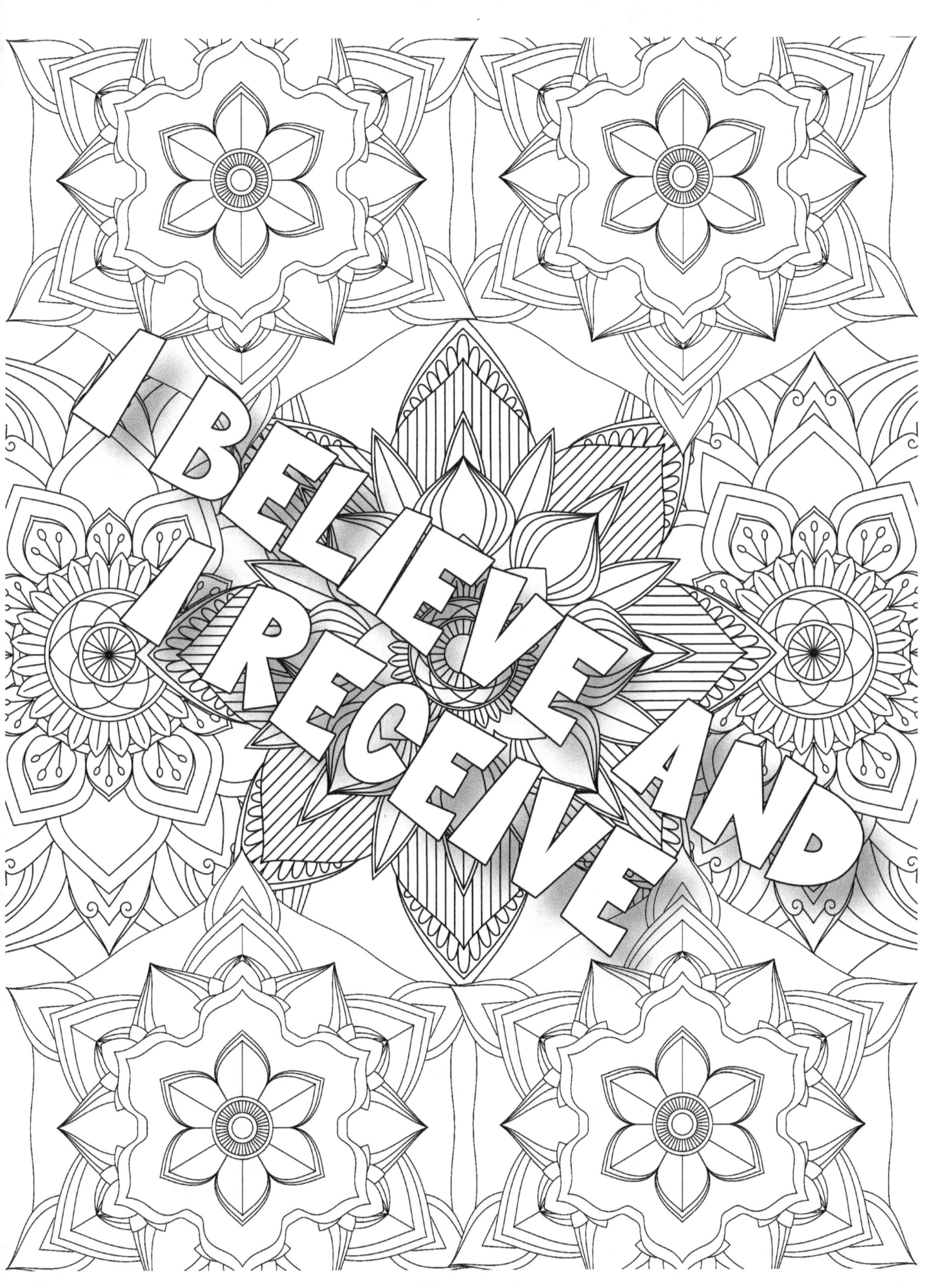

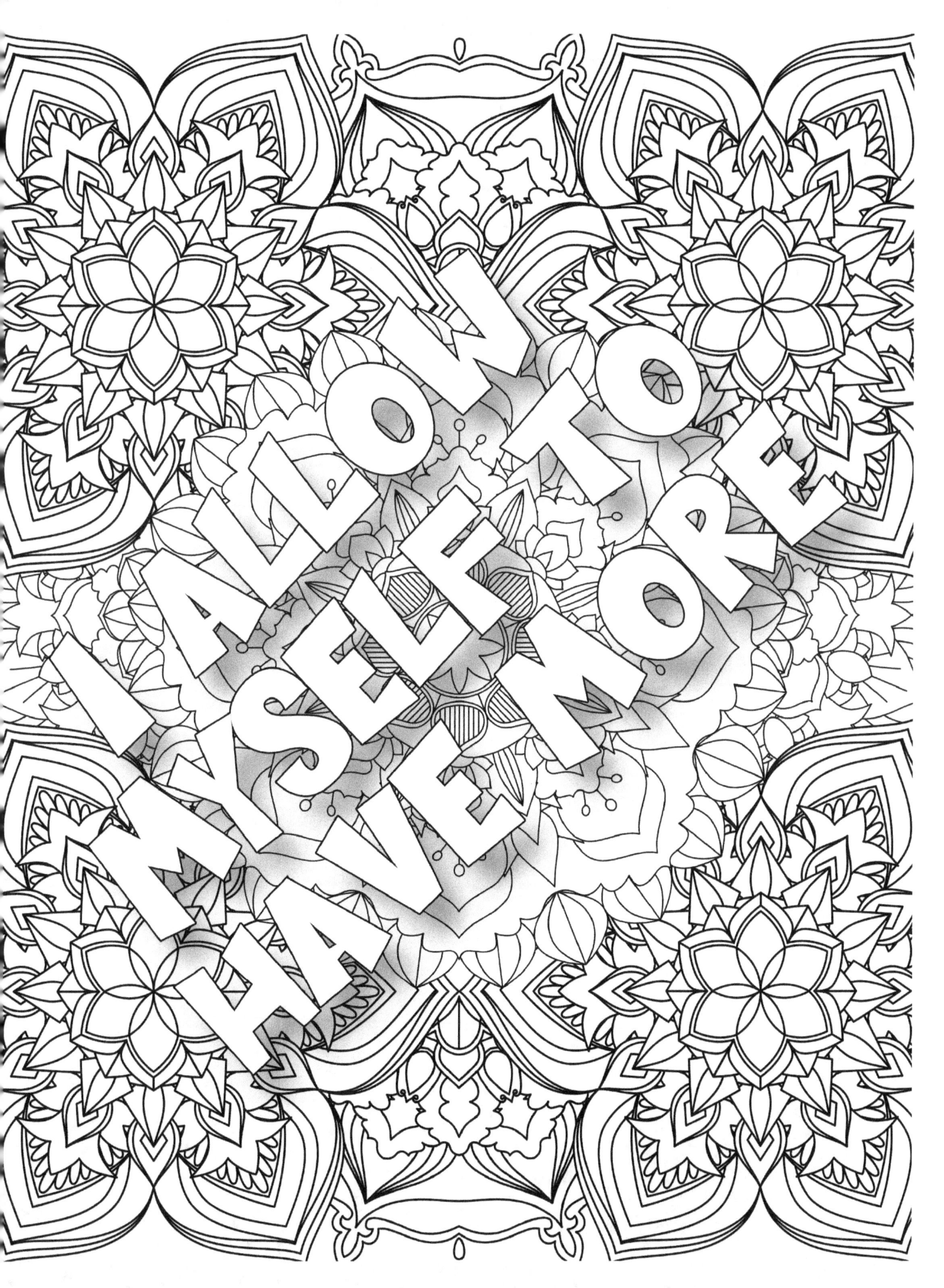

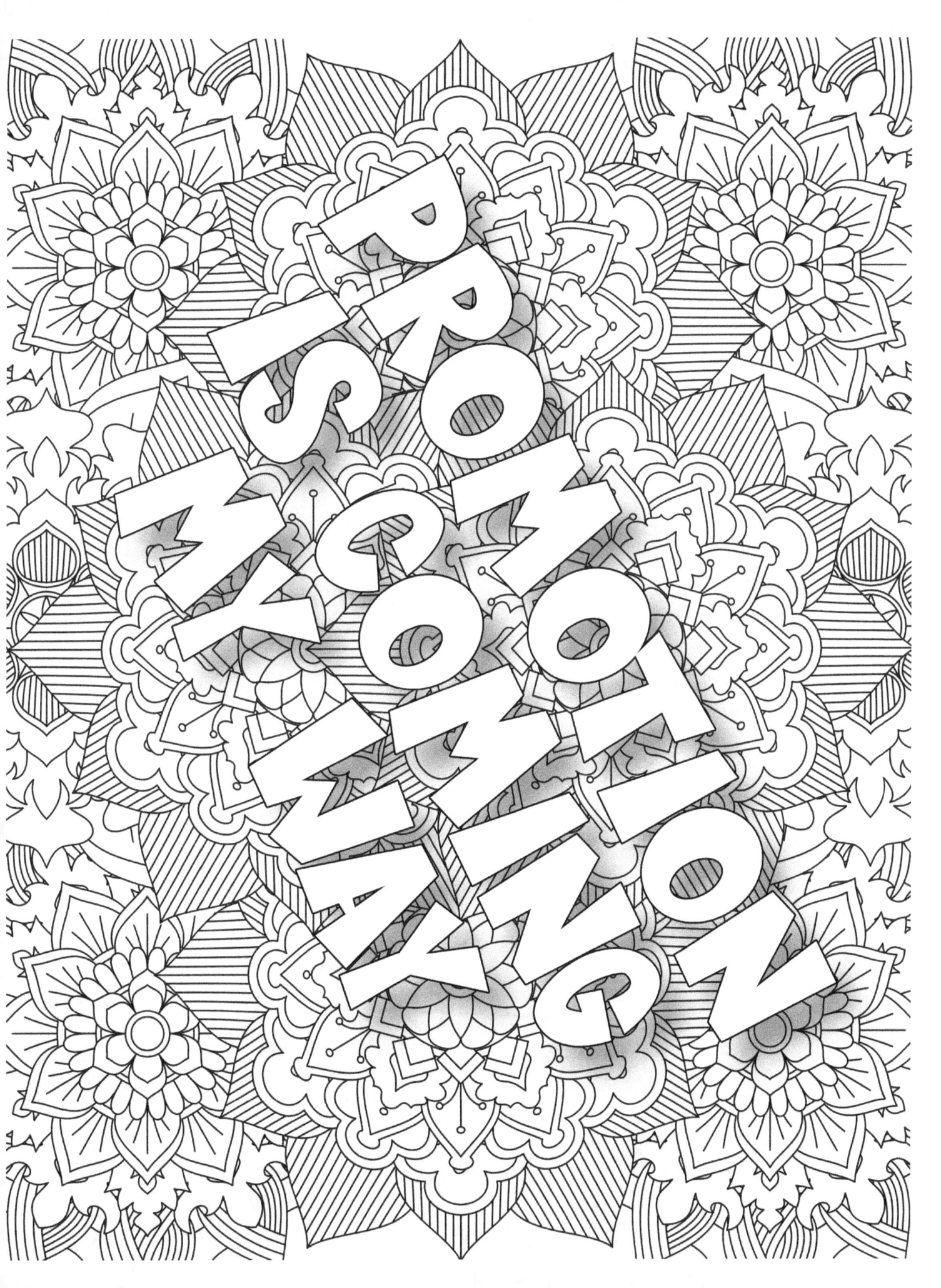

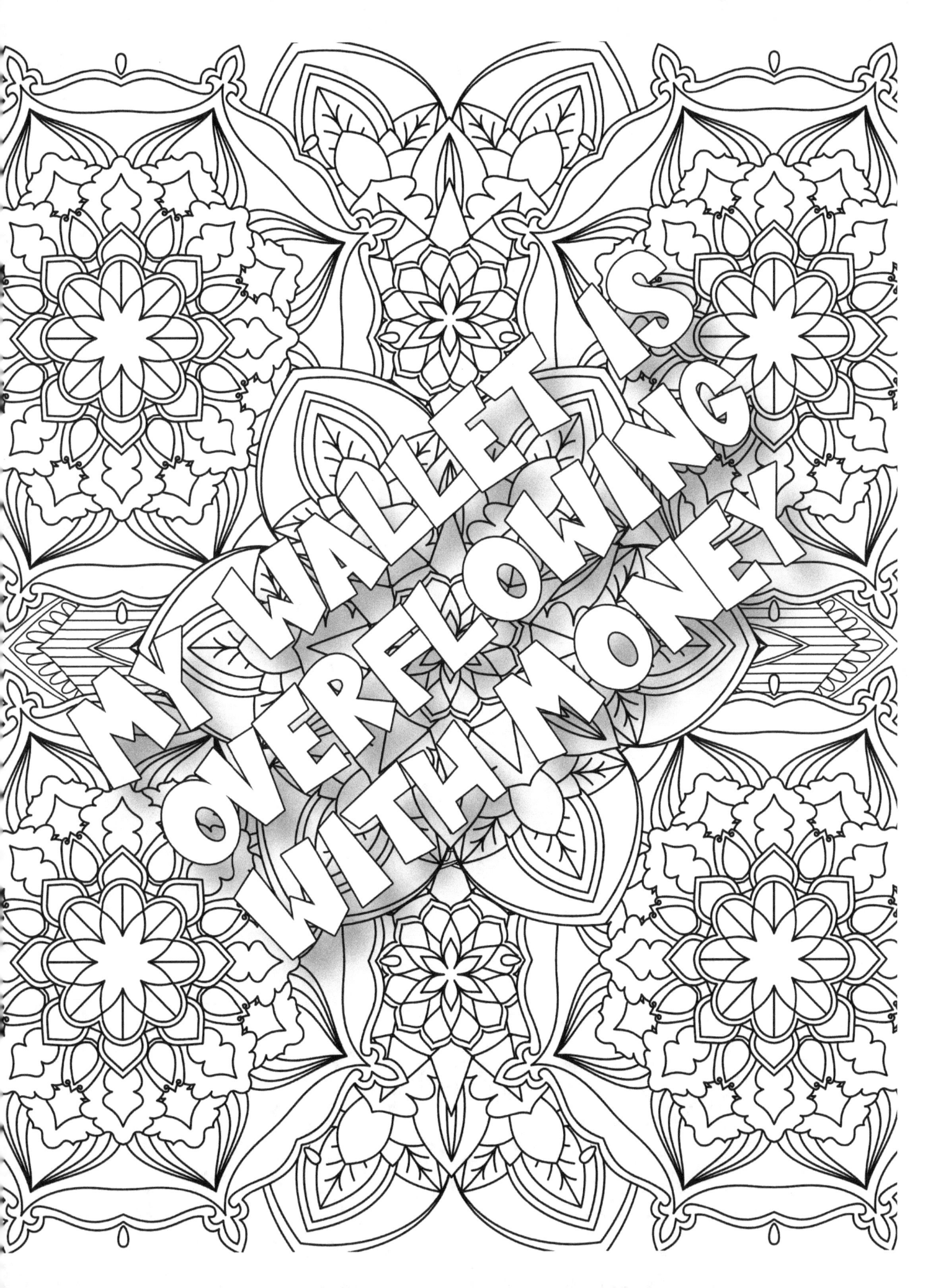

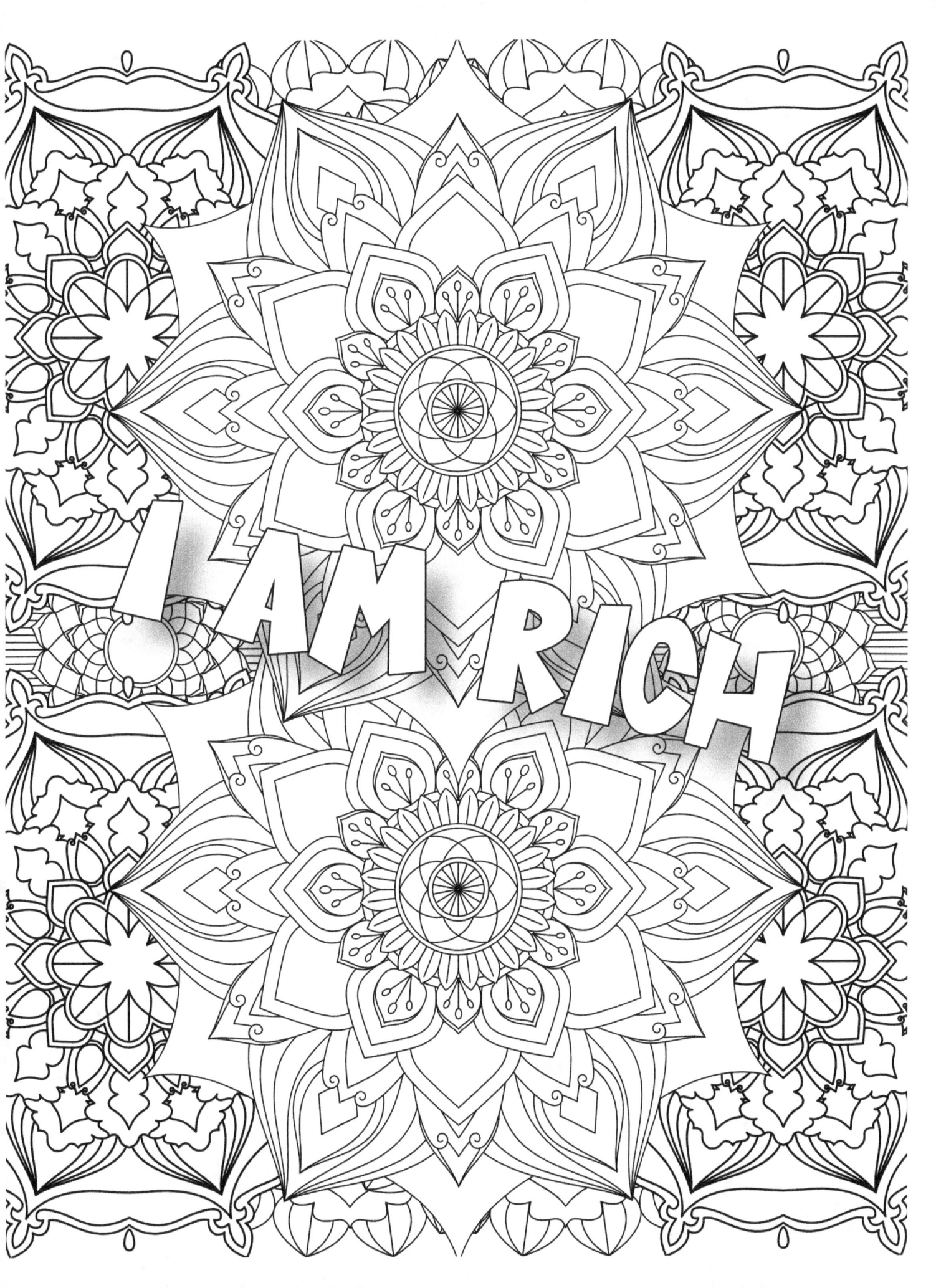

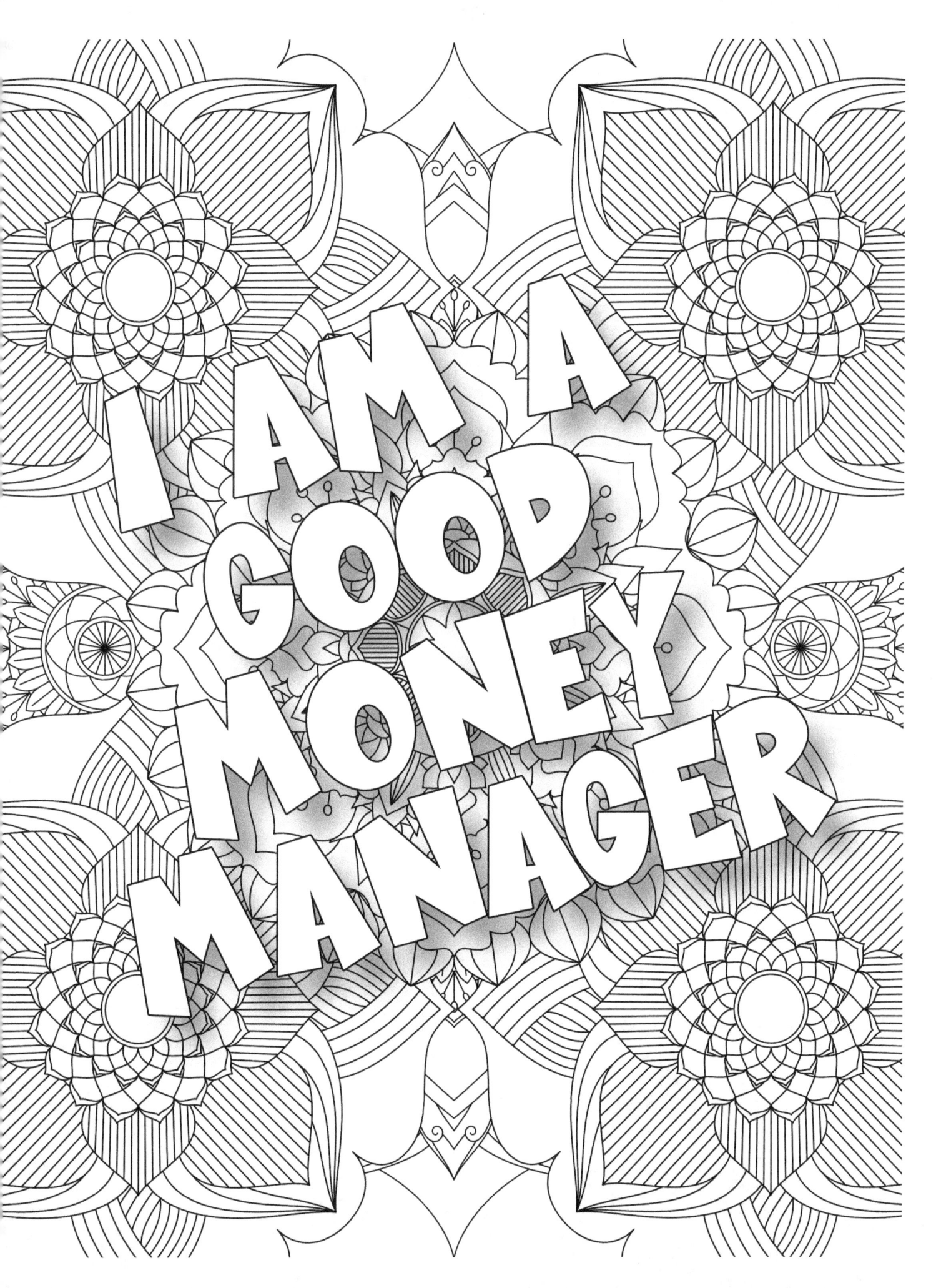

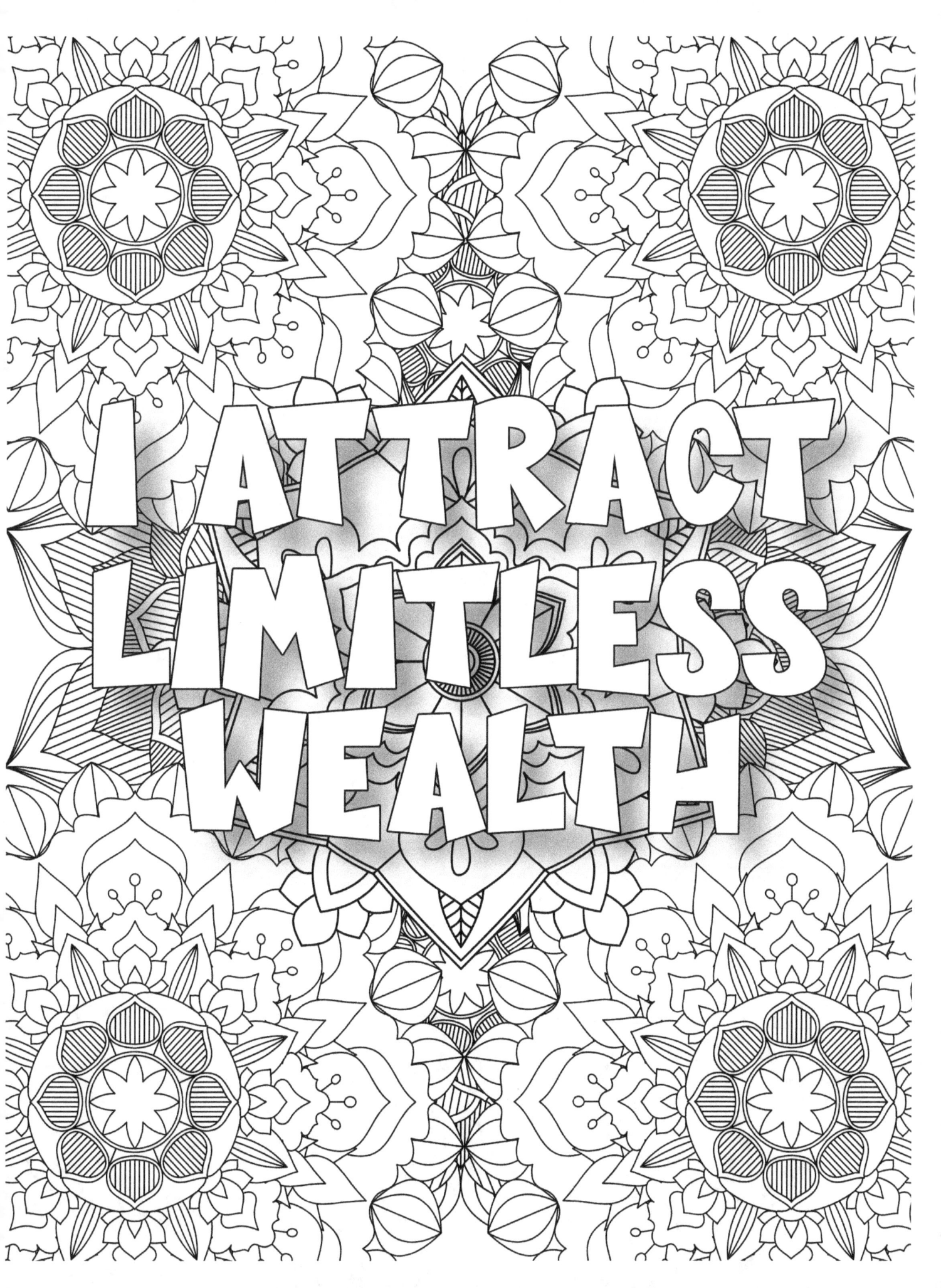

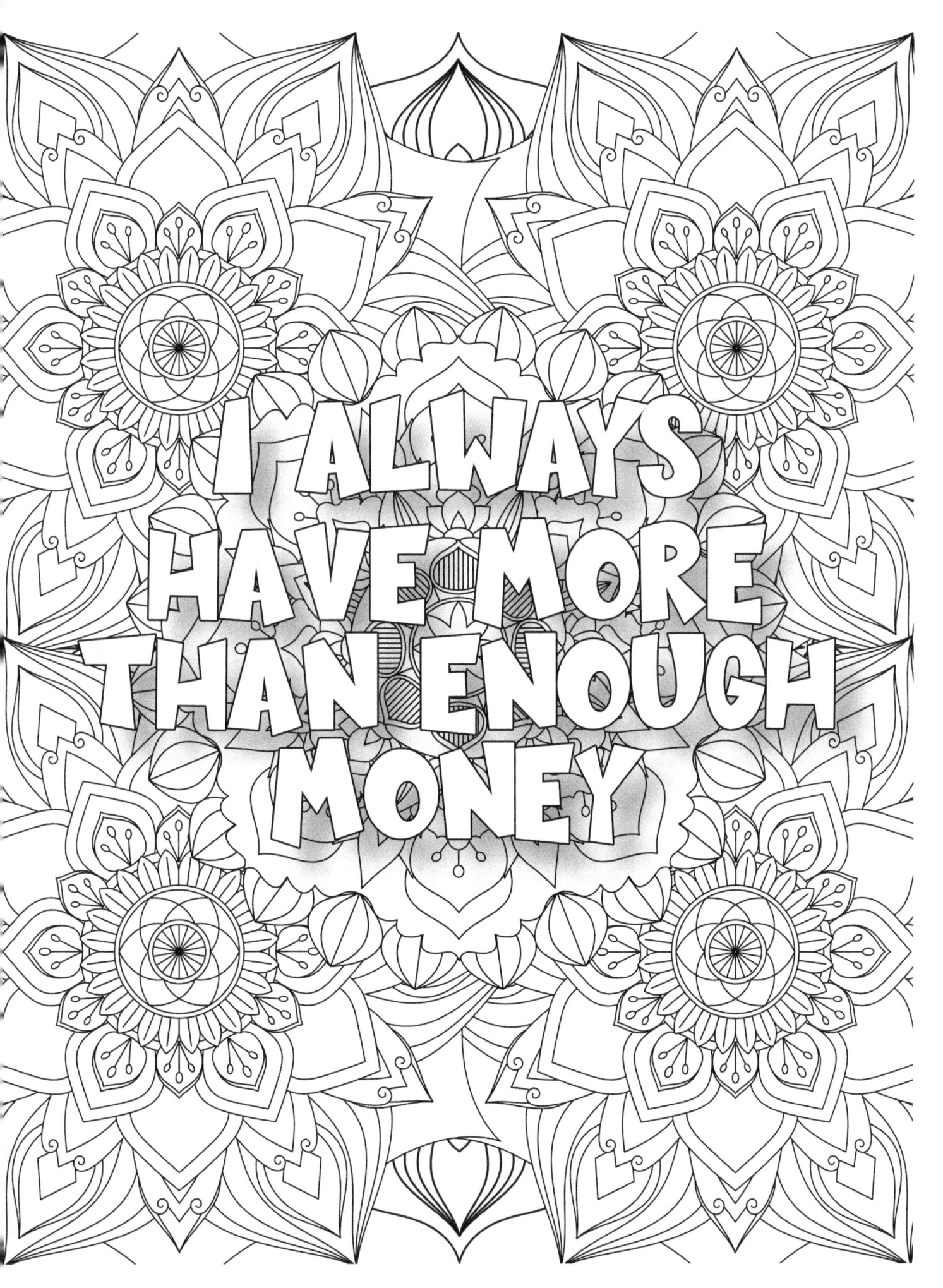

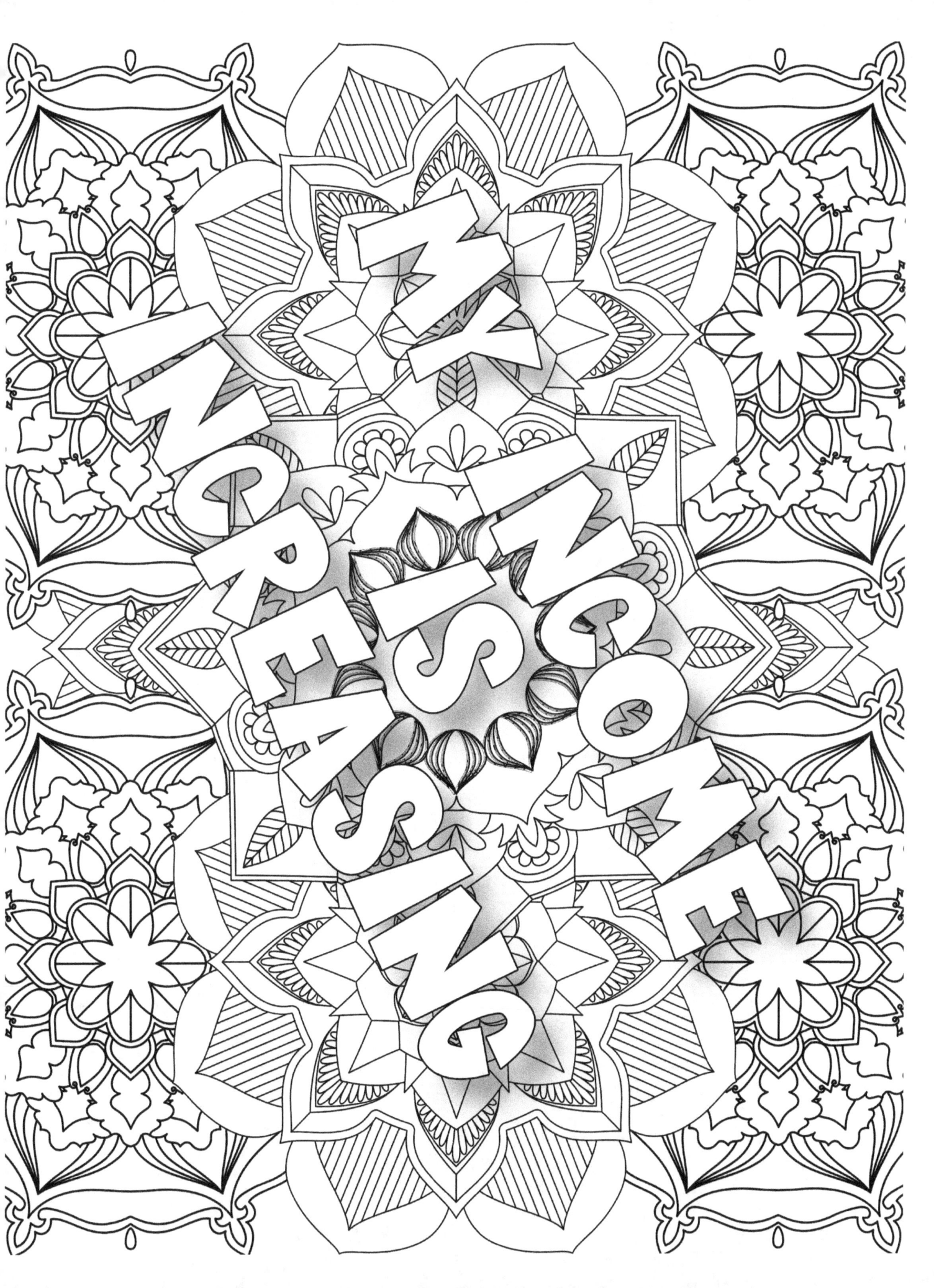

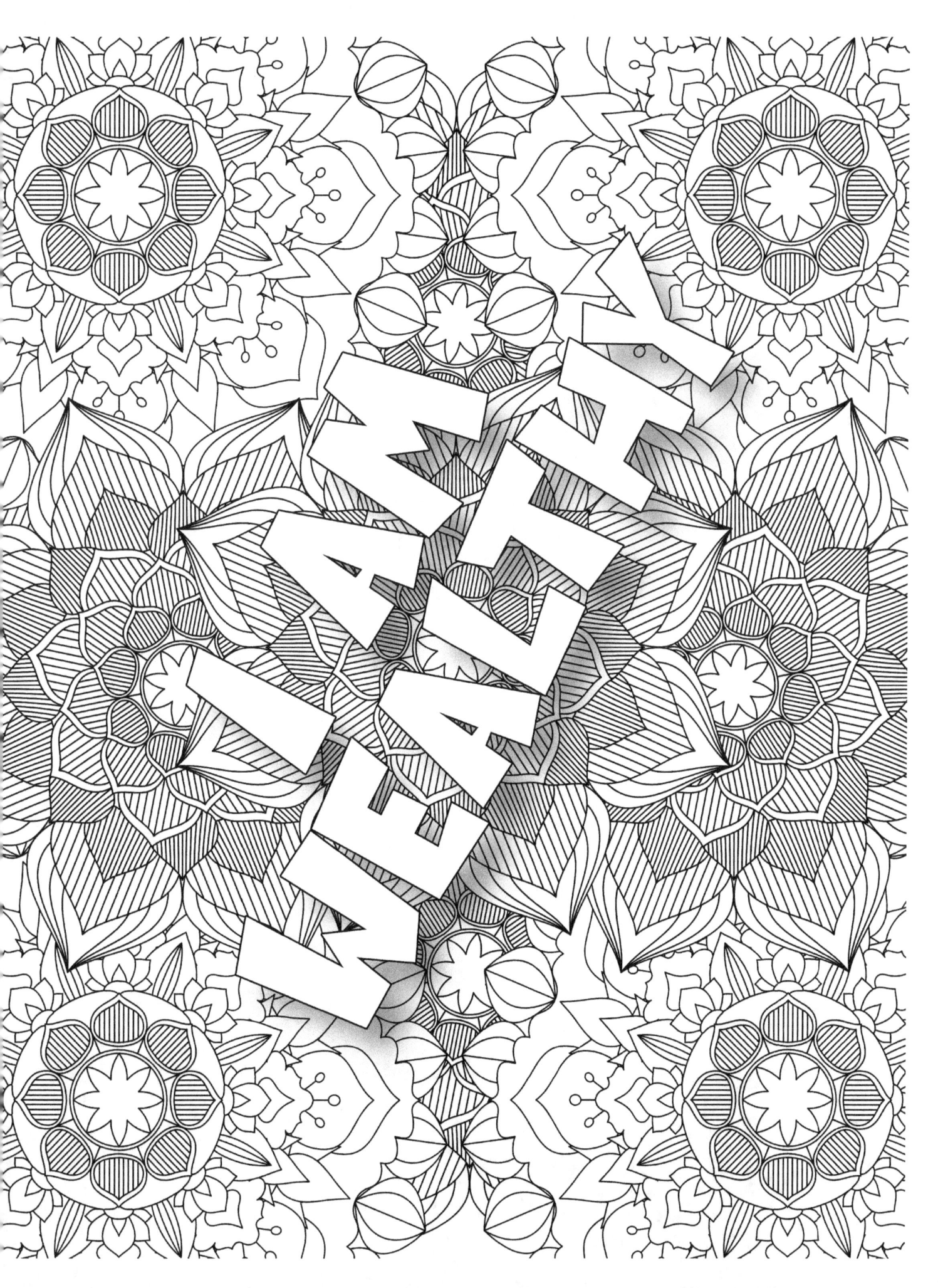

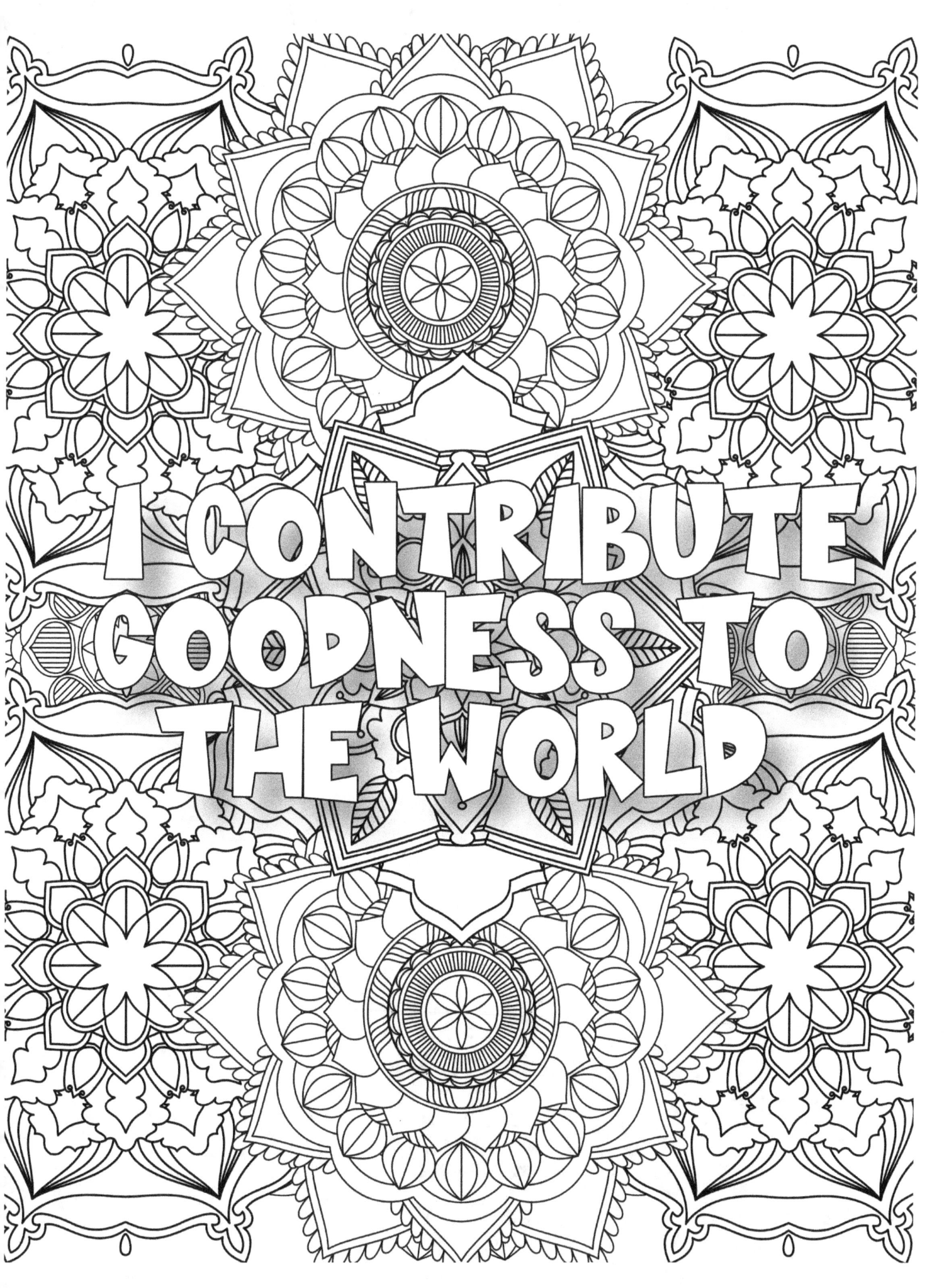

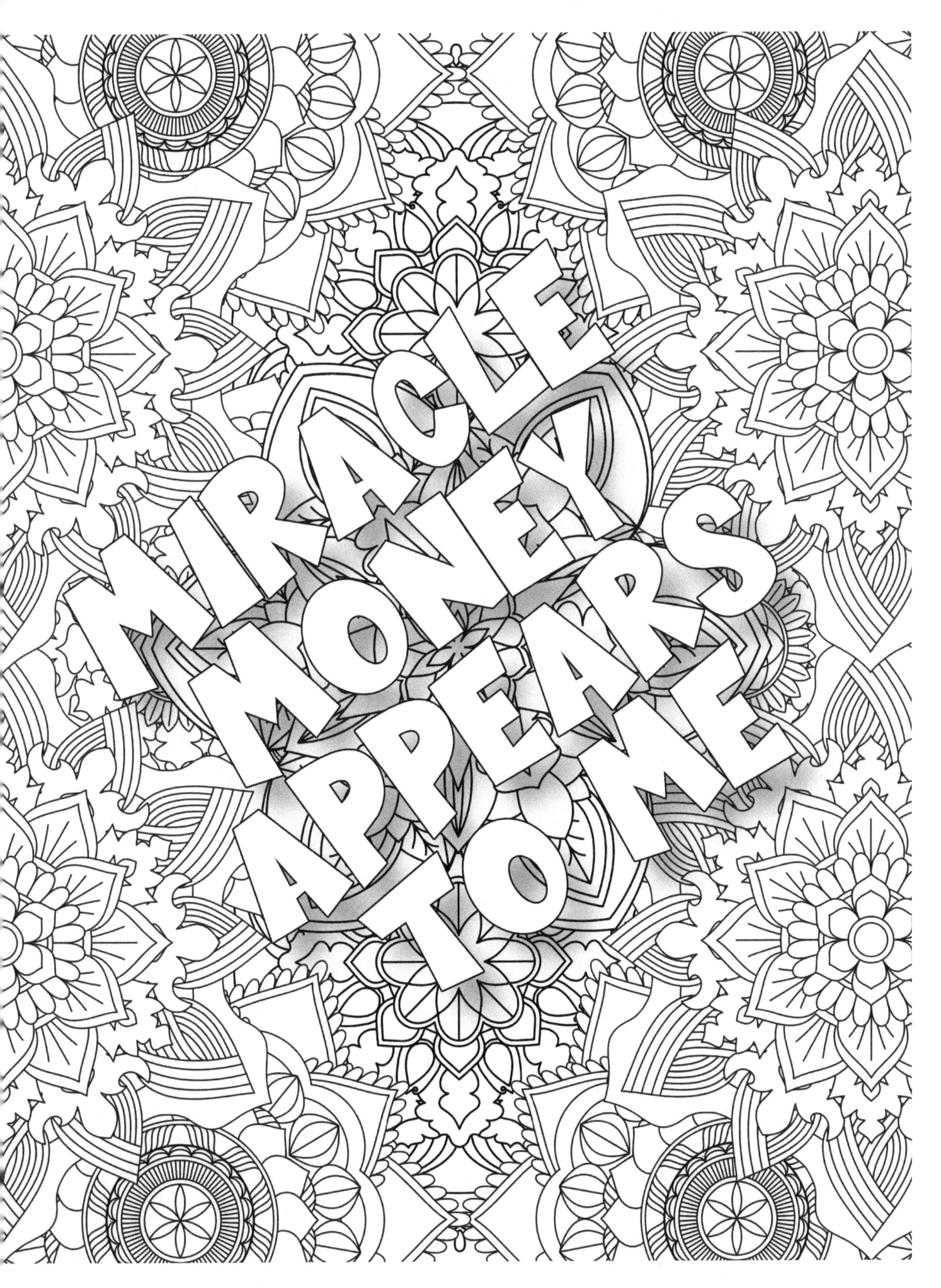

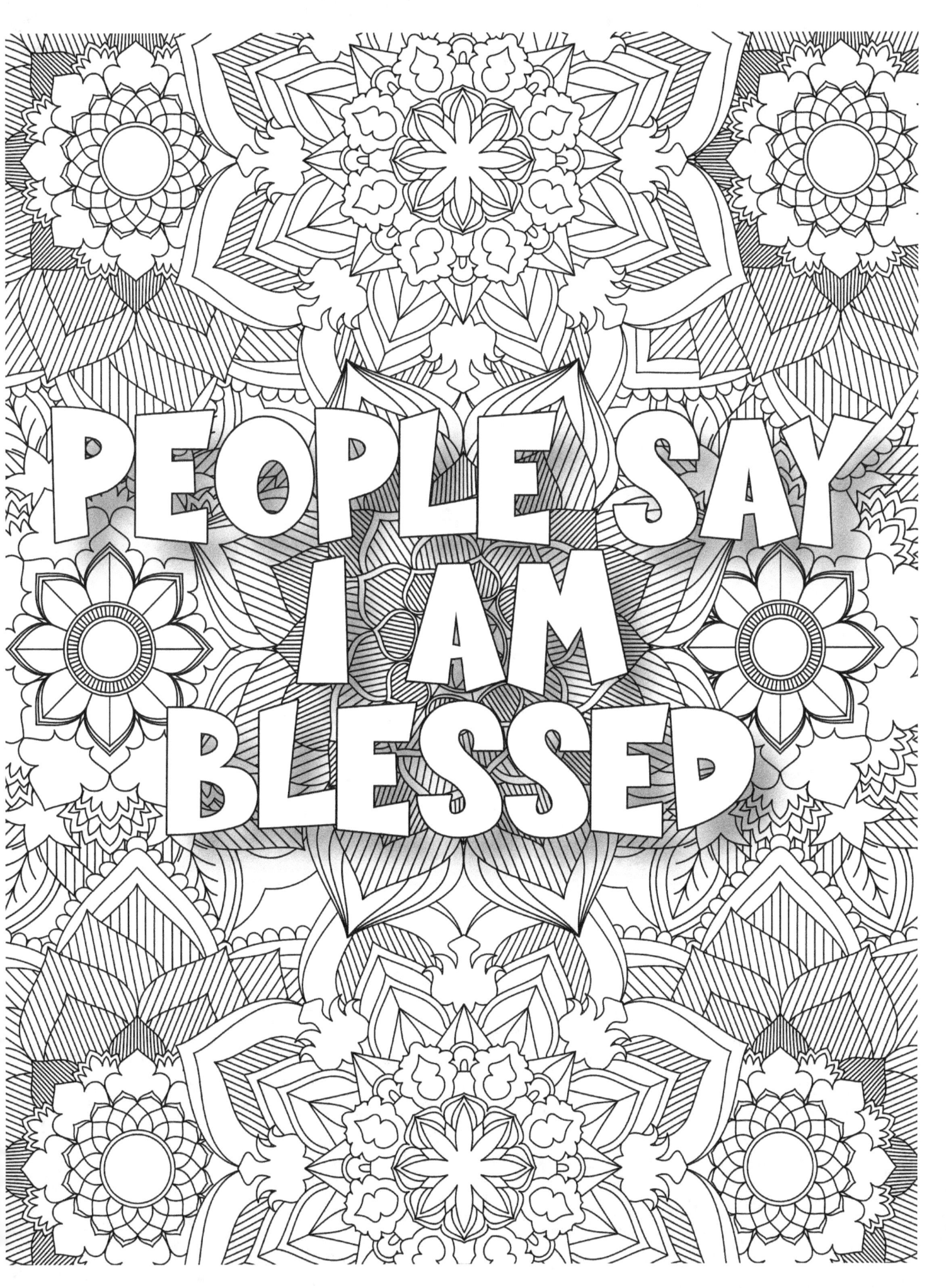

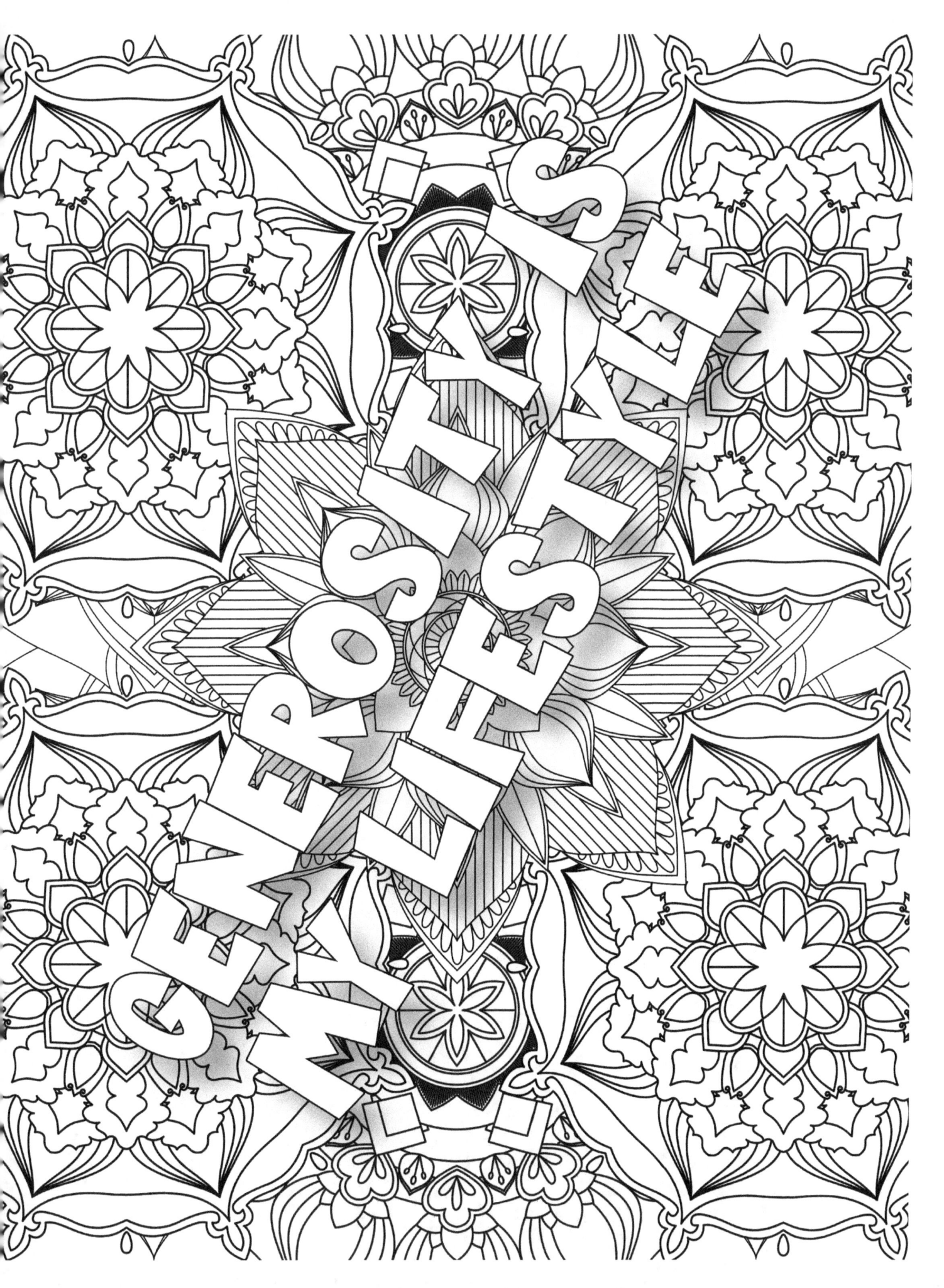

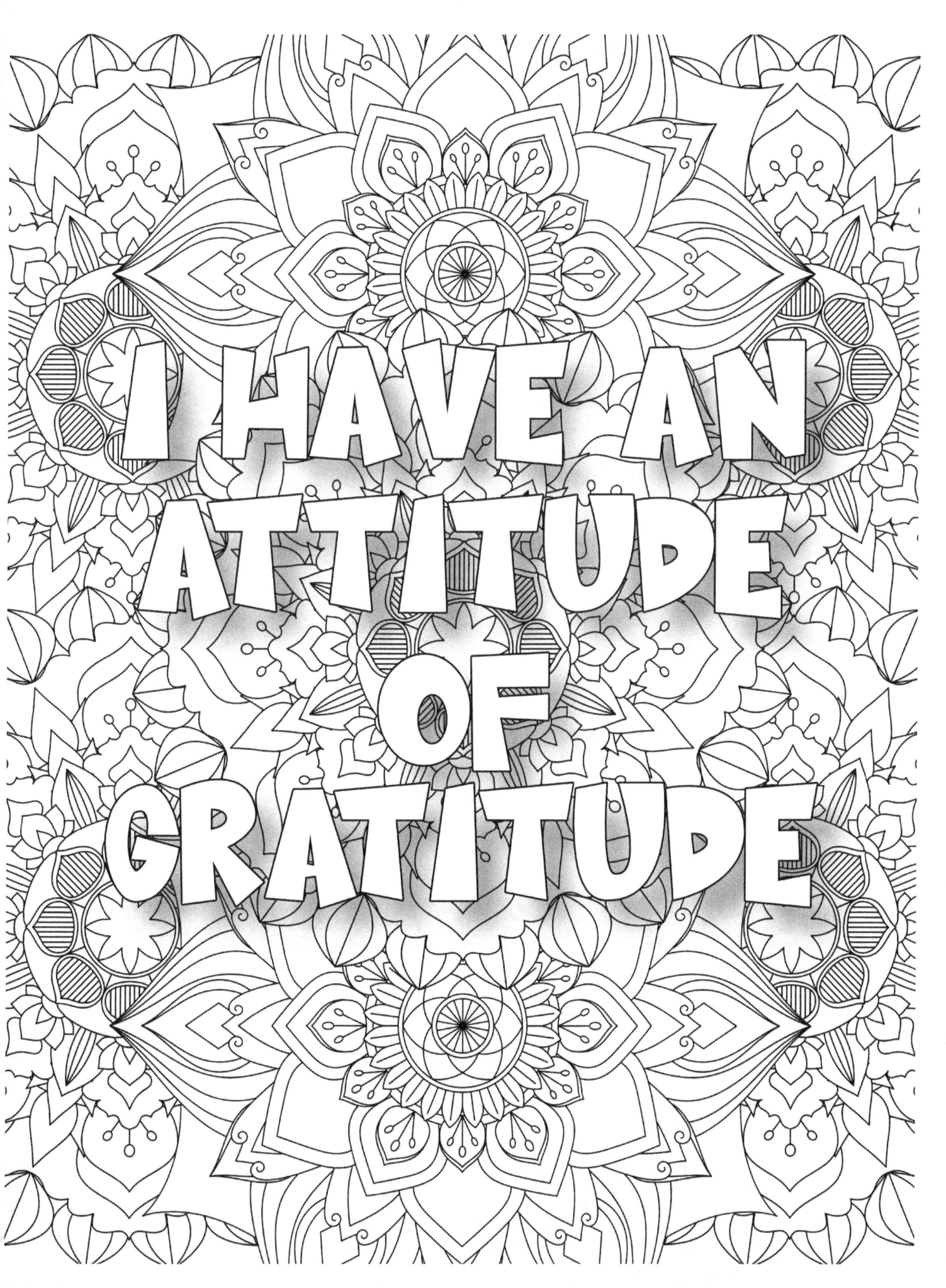

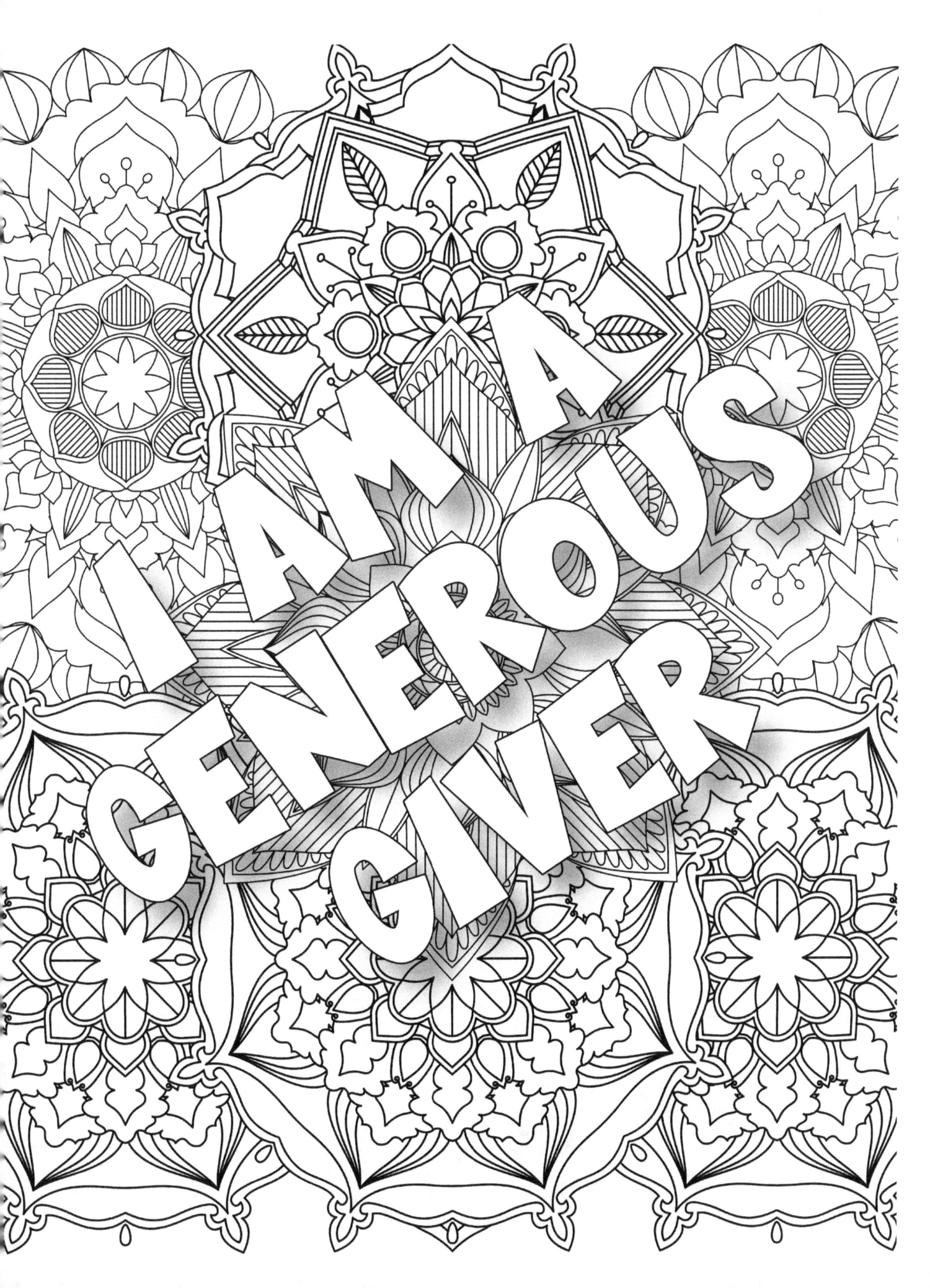

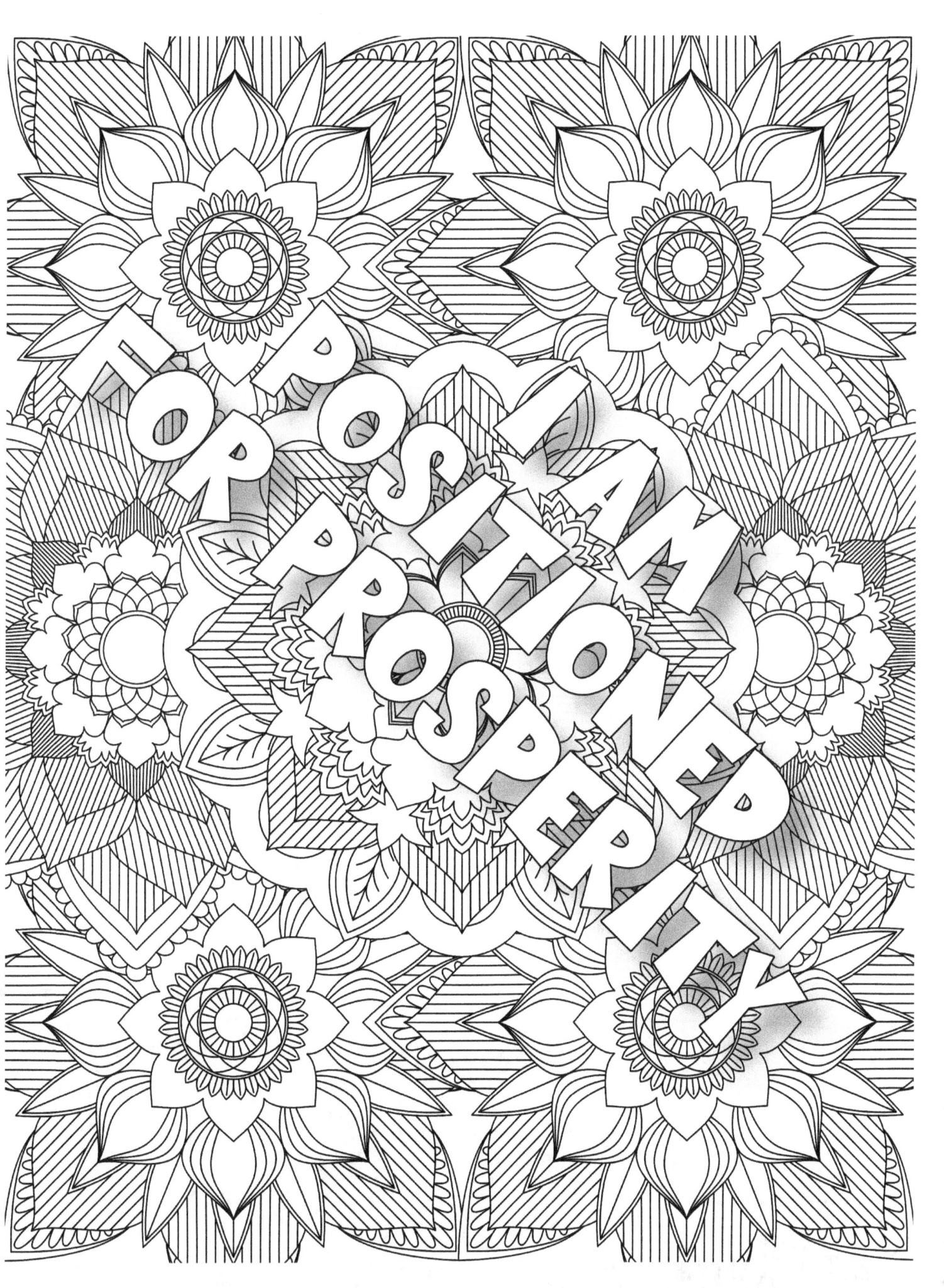

www.ingramcontent.com/pod-product-compliance
Lightning Source LLC
Chambersburg PA
CBHW080910220526
45466CB00011BA/3538